ICE POPS!

50 delicious, fresh and fabulous icy treats

Cesar and Nadia Roden

Photography by Adam Slama
Illustrations by Peter Roden & Divya Scialo

STERLING EPICURE
New York

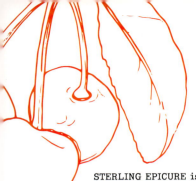

STERLING EPICURE
New York

An Imprint of Sterling Publishing
1166 Avenue of the Americas
New York, NY 10036

STERLING EPICURE is a trademark of Sterling Publishing Co., Inc. The distinctive Sterling logo is a registered trademark of Sterling Publishing Co., Inc.

This Sterling Epicure edition published in 2015

First published in 2014 by Quadrille Publishing Limited
www.quadrille.co.uk

Text © 2014 Cesar and Nadia Roden
Photography © 2014 Adam Slama
Illustrations © 2014 Peter Roden and Divya Scialo, except for endpapers and page 11 designed by Nadia Roden

Publishing Director: Jane O'Shea
Creative Director: Helen Lewis
Senior Editor: Céline Hughes
Designers: Peter Roden, Gemma Hogan
Production: Vincent Smith, Sasha Hawkes

Every effort has been made to trace the customers featured in the photography on pages 7, 10, 12, and 13. We would be pleased to insert an appropriate acknowledgment in any subsequent edition.

All rights reserved. No part of this publication may be reproduced, stored in a retrieval system, or transmitted in any form or by any means (including electronic, mechanical, photocopying, recording, or otherwise) without prior written permission from the publisher.

ISBN 978-1-4549-1626-0

Distributed in Canada by Sterling Publishing
c/o Canadian Manda Group, 664 Annette Street
Toronto, Ontario, Canada M6S 2C8

For information about custom editions, special sales, and premium and corporate purchases, please contact Sterling Special Sales at 800-805-5489 or specialsales@sterlingpublishing.com.

Manufactured in China

2 4 6 8 10 9 7 5 3 1

www.sterlingpublishing.com

CONTENTS

6 Introduction

14 The techniques
16 The basics
Properties of an ice pop ● Tools you'll need
18 The fun part
Fun with molds ● Fun with sticks ● Stripes & swirls
Suspending ingredients ● Decorations & sprinkles ● Serving suggestions
22 The procedure

24 The ice pops
Orange & Lemon ● Raspberry & Lime ● Lemon & Ginger
Blackberry ● Strawberries & Cream ● Tart Plum ● Cantaloupe & Basil
Lychee & Lemongrass ● Drenched Watermelon ● Strawberry & Pepper
Peaches & Cream ● Blueberry & Yogurt ● Apricot & Pistachio
Peach & Tarragon ● Ruby Grapefruit & Campari
Sweet Pear & Ginger ● Cherry & Red Currant
Fresh Mango ● Clementine, White Wine & Rose ● Pineapple & Coconut
Coconut & Lime ● Banana Chocodip ● Cranberry & Orange
Rhubarb & Custard ● White Grapefruit & Star Anise
Egyptian Hibiscus & Peach ● Burgundy Berry ● Mojito
Sweet Sherry & Raisin ● Almond & Orange Blossom ● Pistachio & Rose
Minted Milk ● Three Milks Lemon Dessert ● French Twist
50s Orange Cheesecake ● Milk & Honey ● Cassata ● Butterscotch
Soni's Kulfi ● Cereal Milk ● New York Black & White
Caramel Chocolate ● Mexican Chocolate ● Chocolate & Vanilla Swirl
Chocolate ● Cappuccino ● Vietnamese Coffee
Earl Grey ● Cucumber & Lime ● Beet & Sour Cream

126 Index
128 Acknowledgments

GOOD GOLLY, 50 ICE POPS!

Ice Kitchen was launched in London in spring 2013 with the aim of selling gourmet artisan ice pops. After a fantastic summer on the street, we continued to experiment and explore the endless possibilities of an ice pop. This is a collection of our favorite recipes that can easily be made at home and that you can enjoy throughout the year on every kind of occasion.

On the following pages you will find our aunt and nephew story, from its beginning in New York to the streets of London.

Be sure to take a look at the Techniques section before you start on your ice pop journey—there are lots of useful tips!

ICE POP HEAVEN, FROM NY TO LONDON

In the summer of 2009, in Woodstock, New York, I came across a photo of a transparent ice pop with a leaf frozen inside it. It looked so beautiful and it immediately sparked my imagination, which started running wild with all sorts of flavors and concoctions that could be frozen in ice. I thought it was such a playful and unique idea and I couldn't help myself from pursuing it. I'm an artist and always open to new ideas; I can also get a little obsessed!

While my two-year-old daughter Lily slept, I filled sketchbooks with ideas for flavor combinations and turned our kitchen into a lab. I filled our SoHo loft with freezers and a special machine from Latin America and experimented with all sorts of flavors and textures. The challenge was how to get the best out of each ingredient, to allow its natural characteristics to shine in ice. I found that often the pairing of two flavors could bring out the best in both and I was particularly happy when I found simple combinations that worked, like oranges and lemons, or milk and honey. Herbs and spices could complement and add complexity to a fruit, like basil with cantaloupe melon, or star anise with grapefruit. A touch of lemon or lime of ten intensified the flavor. I was also inspired by childhood favorites that my mother Claudia (Cesar's grandmother) had made, like a pistachio and rose milk dessert, which I reconstructed as an ice pop; others were inspired by classics from around the world, like the Spanish sherry with raisin, or the Sicilian cassata.

I enrolled in an ice-cream course at a university and kept the ice pop plan a secret. I found a beautiful stainless-steel street cart and painted black and white polka dots on it and a 1920s flapper called Lily Lolly, running with a bunch of ice pops: she represented a free spirit, which is what this endeavor felt like to me. I called the business Lily Lolly's Ice Kitchen. My stepmother, Peggy, who lives in New York, was such a big help all along the way, getting all the licenses and the commercial kitchen and finding us our launch spot at Herald Square, right next to Macy's.

Our first spot at Herald Square was a disaster! The crowds were too thick and we had to push our heavy cart 25 blocks to and from our kitchen through heavy traffic in 100°F heat every day! Our first customer was a police car—we thought he'd stopped to tell us off, but it was to buy an ice pop. Then, another time, four police cars stopped at Herald Square and took our cart away with a crane to the police department. It was a mistake of course! But all our ice pops melted in the meantime.

I was relieved and overjoyed when my nephew Cesar then arrived from London to help me. Apart from being a whiz at the cart, he has amazing taste and we worked together in the kitchen. After being offered a spot at the weekly Bryant Park Film Festival, word started to spread and the High Line Park, an overhead railroad line transformed into a park in the sky above Manhattan, called us to ask for our cart! A great mix of people passed by every day and it was surreal to see so many of them holding our ice pops as they strolled along the amazing garden, and wonderful to see the reactions as they tasted them. The queues at our cart were now winding along the promenade!

Cesar and I kept coming up with new flavors and to keep up with the huge demand on the High Line, I spent months in the kitchen often up until midnight. Then, unfortunately, Cesar was unable to extend his visa and had to return to London.

The next summer I put the project on ice—I wanted to devote more time to my daughter Lily. She would only be this young once and I didn't want to miss all the precious summertimes with her. Meanwhile, Cesar was sure the gourmet ice pops would work as well in London despite the British weather. So when he called to say he was ready, I was very excited and sent him our cart, the blast freezer, and some recipes. He named it simply Ice Kitchen and his brother Peter designed the new graphics and logo; mine had been too feminine with the polka dots and flapper and all! I'm blown away by Cesar's vision and what he's achieved with Ice Kitchen in its first summer in London. I'm so proud of him!

This book is a collaboration and a collection of recipes from the New York and London experiences plus many more we created during a winter of experimenting and testing.

Nadia Roden

ICE KITCHEN IS BORN

I started my first food venture with my school friend Liam. We sold coffee, chocolate, and ice cream at various markets around London from our three-wheeled Piaggio coffee van. It was a great experience, but in the end we didn't get the best spots and we ended up selling the van.

After returning from New York I really wanted to show London the special gourmet ice pops, as I knew nobody else was making them like this, and I hoped this would make it easier to get the market pitches and events. I turned the upstairs kitchen of my parents' house into the Ice Kitchen with the specialized equipment Nadia had sent, and immediately started experimenting. I kept thinking of the crazy amount of labor that had been involved in New York: cooking, churning, swirling, dipping in chocolate, sprinkling with nuts, wrapping, labeling, and packing. But I was eager to get out and show London how good an ice pop could be! Eventually, the whole house was filled with freezers and carts and crates of fruit and I was driving my parents crazy!

My first event was on the South Bank on the Easter weekend, and it started snowing. I only sold ten ice pops, and most people laughed

as I stood there shivering, trying not to scare off potential customers. I wondered if I'd made the right decision, but luckily the weather turned into one of the hottest summers on record and I started coming home with an empty cart and a suntan!

Eating in the street has become so popular and streetfood culture and events have become huge in London. I joined Kerb, a collective of streetfood traders that "make cities taste better" by popping up at locations around London and by hosting events of their own. They are really supportive, with a genuine community vibe that cares about good food. I love being a part of the streetfood community and the instant feedback you get from the customers!

My best pitch is at the South Bank Real Food market; I think there's no better place to be on a summer evening, enjoying a mojito ice pop as you walk by the river.

I had fun working with Nadia in the kitchen—she is a real ice wizard at creating imaginative ice pops! This book truly was a family affair and we've been so lucky to have so many creative family members on board. My brother Peter designed the cover and artwork along with his girlfriend Divya whose illustrations are throughout, and our friend Adam stepped in to photograph every one of the ice pops. Our families have loved all of the recipes in this book and we hope you will too.

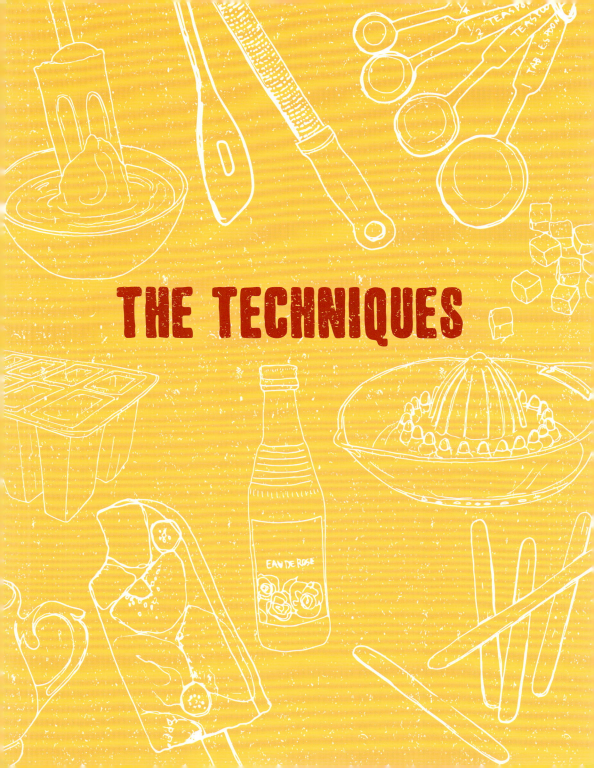

THE TECHNIQUES

THE BASICS
PROPERTIES OF AN ICE POP

A pinch of salt can enhance the flavor, even for a fruit pop.

Ice pop mixtures are not churned like in ice creams or sorbets, so their texture is icy and melts quickly in your mouth.

Freezing diminishes sweetness, so make your mixture a little sweeter than you might like. We usually use natural granulated sugar but other sweeteners such as brown sugar, honey, agave syrup, maple syrup, or Stevia all work fine. Syrups and honeys make smoother, softer ice pops.

A tiny amount of alcohol gives a nice soft texture but too much prevents the ice pop from freezing, as it has a low freezing point (2-5 tablespoons per 10 ice pops is sufficient). One great idea is to dip ice pops in alcohol, e.g. rum, vodka, Campari, gin, or whisky.

Infusing a base syrup with herbs and spices can complement and add complexity to different fruits. However, spices taste spicier when frozen, so use a light touch.

Choose the freshest, ripest seasonal fruits. We use a touch of lemon or lime in almost all our fruity ice pops as it heightens the flavor. When using citrus zest, use a fine zester and zest only the colored part of the peel, avoiding the bitter white pith.

Use fresh whole milk, cream, and yogurt as well as good-quality chocolate, tea, nuts, herbs, spices, and flowers.

TOOLS YOU'LL NEED

Kitchen scale

Strong blender or food processor to puree fruit

Measuring spoons

Fine-mesh strainer to strain out solids, such as seeds

Small or medium saucepan to make simple syrups, cook fruit, or heat milk

Juicer for juicing lemons and oranges

Cutting board and knife for cutting up fruit, nuts, and chocolate

Fine zester for zesting lemon and orange peel

Ice pop mold (see page 18)

Ice pop sticks

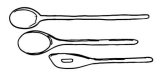

Heatproof spatula or wooden spoon for stirring a mixture over heat or through a strainer

THE FUN PART

FUN WITH MOLDS

There are many ready-made molds to choose from in different shapes and sizes, and made from plastic, metal, or silicone. For all the recipes in this book, a 10 x 2.5-oz. (70-ml) ice pop mold was used and yielded 8 to 10 ice pops. You can also buy expensive ice pop makers that will freeze an ice pop in just 15 minutes. Be creative and use other containers as molds, such as small wax-lined paper cups, shot glasses, tall thin glasses, or even ice-cube trays. Just make sure that the top of the mold isn't narrower than the bottom, otherwise you won't be able to pull the frozen pop out!

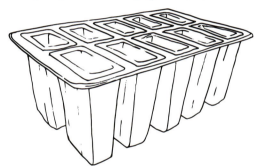

FUN WITH STICKS

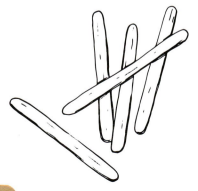

Wooden sticks are the best, as the ice pop will stick firmly to them. You should buy them in large quantities—they're cheap and you'll have lots on hand. You can also be inventive and use clean twigs, bamboo, or cinnamon sticks, and even a toothpick in an ice-cube tray will work. To keep the sticks in place, it's a good idea to cover the tops of the molds with foil and cut a little slit where you want the stick, then insert the stick through the foil.

STRIPES & SWIRLS

To layer flavors in stripes, simply partially freeze the first layer before adding the next, and so on. It takes a little extra time (you should wait at least 30 to 60 minutes per layer) but it's fun for a special occasion. Add the stick after the second or third layer. To create an angled stripe, just prop your mold up on a bag of frozen peas so the mixture inside freezes at an angle and people will wonder how you did it!

To make swirls, pour alternate layers of two thick mixtures, or of one thin and one thick mixture into the mold and swizzle it a little with an ice pop stick before freezing.

SUSPENDING INGREDIENTS

Chunks of fruit, little berries, nuts, chocolate pieces, edible flowers, herbs, and many other ingredients can be suspended in an ice pop if the mixture is thick. If the mixture is thin, fill the mold halfway and freeze it a little before mixing in the suspended ingredient—this will prevent it from sinking to the bottom. You can even skewer some ingredients onto the sticks as a hidden surprise.

DECORATIONS & SPRINKLES

- Place coconut flakes, chopped nuts, seeds, or cookie crumbs onto a plate or in a communal bowl on the table and roll and press the frozen ice pops into them.

- Sprinkle ground spices, such as cinnamon, cayenne, or cocoa onto the frozen ice pops.

- To coat an ice pop in chocolate, make sure the ice pop is frozen hard. Put $3\frac{1}{2}$ ounces chocolate and 1 tablespoon vegetable or coconut oil (the oil prevents the chocolate from cracking when frozen) in a heatproof bowl set over a saucepan of gently simmering water. Stir the chocolate until melted and smooth (and stir in chopped nuts or coconut or flavorings such as orange zest at this stage if you like). Remove from the heat and let cool to room temperature. To coat an ice pop in chocolate, make sure the ice pop is frozen hard before dipping it in. You can refreeze it on waxed paper until firm, or eat it straightaway.

- To coat an ice pop in toasted nuts, preheat the oven to 350°F. Spread nuts or coconut (dry unsweetened or flaked) on a cookie sheet and toast, turning with a spoon once or twice, for up to 10 minutes until lightly tanned. Cool and chop if needed.

SERVING SUGGESTIONS

You may want to make an impression with how you serve your ice pops for a special occasion. They look beautiful served on a tray of ice cubes or cracked ice and you can decorate the ice with cut fruit, berries, flowers, or floating candles. Alternatively, rest them in a bowl filled with ice and stick in some sparklers!

How about offering a separate or communal dipping bowl with toasted coconut flakes, chopped nuts, or melted chocolate (see opposite). You can also offer individual glasses of alcohol to dip the ice pops into, like rum, vodka, or Prosecco.

The festive season
Layered ice pops of different fruits, flavors, and colors can be made to celebrate occasions, for instance, red, white, and blue, strawberry, vanilla, and blackberry for Independence Day, or cranberry red for Christmas.

Weddings or romantic evenings
Edible flowers and herbs look beautiful inside an ice pop (page 19).

After dinner
Burgundy Berry or Sweet Sherry & Raisin are good after-dinner delicacies. At the end of a heavy meal, Clementine, White Wine & Rose, Cucumber & Lime, or White Grapefruit & Star Anise are better.

Cocktail parties
Mojito, Ruby Grapefruit & Campari, or Drenched Watermelon are good and most fruit-based ice pops can be dipped into a cocktail.

Outdoor activities
Ice pops are a perfect choice for garden parties, picnics, and barbecues (see page 23 for advice on transporting them).

Children
Kids love Milk & Honey, Orange & Lemon, Cherry & Red Currant, Cereal Milk, Minted Milk, 50s Orange Cheesecake, or Chocolate. That's what our Lily Roden likes!

THE PROCEDURE
ESSENTIAL TIPS

1 Fill the molds
When you pour the mixture into the ice pop molds, leave about ¼ inch at the top to let the mixture expand as it freezes. See also page 18.

2 Insert the sticks
Some molds have a metal tray through which you can insert the sticks. If so, make sure the sticks go in straight, otherwise you'll have a really hard time taking the metal tray off when you are ready to unmold the ice pops. We prefer to use this method: leave the molds uncovered in the freezer for about 1 hour (but be careful not to forget them—we've done it many times!), then insert the sticks and they will remain upright. Alternatively, use the foil trick (see page 18).

3 Freeze
Turn your freezer to the coldest setting. The faster the ice pop freezes, the smaller the ice crystals will be, which means it will be creamier. Put your molds at the back of the freezer where it's coldest. Ice pops take 4 to 8 hours to freeze, depending on the ingredients you use. The higher the water-to-sugar ratio the faster your ice pop will freeze. Alcohol will slow the process and too much will result in a slushy ice pop. There are some expensive instant ice pop makers that will freeze an ice pop in just 15 minutes, so that's an option if you're really impatient.

4. Unmold
Carefully immerse the molds in hot water (we use the kitchen sink) for about 10 to 20 seconds, making sure to dip them right up to just below the top rim, then pull hard on the sticks to yank them out. If they don't come out, they might need a second immersion. If you are using individual molds, you can run hot water over the outside of the mold and then pull hard on the sticks.

5. Eat or store
Enjoy your ice pops immediately or store them in sealable freezer bags or waxed paper bags in the freezer. Make sure they are airtight to prevent ice crystals from forming inside and a taste of "freezer burn." You can also keep them frozen in their molds until you are ready to eat them, but try not to leave them for too long because they taste much better within a week of making.

6. Transport
Use insulated freezer bags or a Styrofoam container or ice chest, if you ever need to transport ice pops. The more ice pops you transport together, the longer they will stay frozen. For a very long trip you may want to purchase a block of dried ice, which will keep them frozen for many hours.

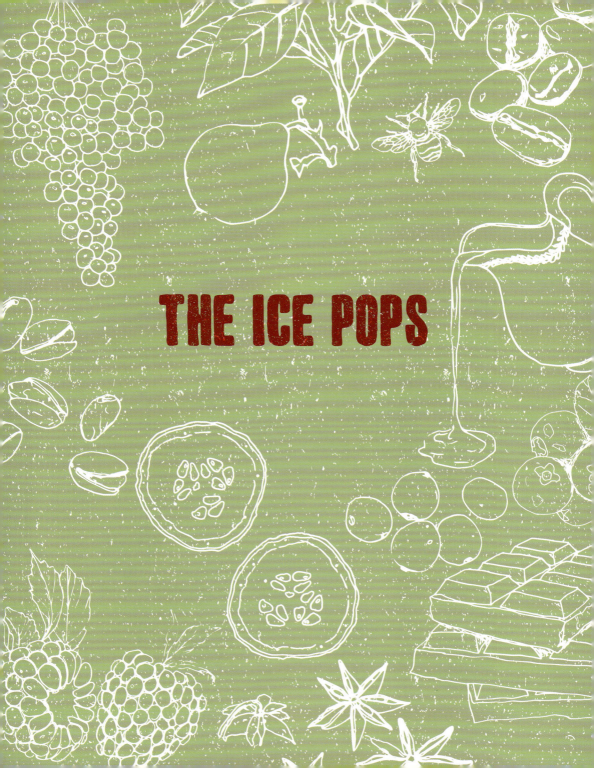

ORANGE & LEMON

This is one of the simplest and most thirst-quenching combinations there is and it's bursting with flavor. The taste is so much better if you choose the freshest sweet-tasting oranges and squeeze them yourself.

- finely grated zest of 1 orange
- ¼ cup plus 2 tablespoons granulated sugar
- 4 tablespoons water
- 2½ cups freshly squeezed orange juice (from about 6 oranges)
- ⅓ cup freshly squeezed lemon juice (from about 3 lemons)

Put the orange zest, sugar, and water in a small saucepan and bring to a simmer. Simmer until the sugar has dissolved, then stir the syrup into the orange and lemon juices.

Pour the mixture into your icepop molds, leaving ¼-inch at the top to let the mixture expand when it freezes. Insert the ice pop sticks and freeze. (See page 22 for the complete procedure.)

RASPBERRY & LIME

This is sweet and tangy with a subtle undercurrent of lime. We don't strain out the raspberry seeds for the carts and most people have no problem with that—in fact they love the realness of it. But if you prefer a smooth, silky texture we recommend straining the mixture through a fine strainer.

- generous 1 cup granulated sugar
- finely grated zest of 1 lime
- 1¼ cups water
- 4 cups raspberries, rinsed
- 2-3 tablespoons freshly squeezed lime juice

Put the sugar, lime zest, and scant ½ cup of the water in a small saucepan and bring to a simmer. Simmer until the sugar has dissolved.

Put the raspberries in a food processor with the lime syrup and the remaining water and blend to a puree. Add 2 tablespoons of the lime juice and taste to see if it's sharp enough. If not, add a little more to achieve an equal balance of sweet and sharp.

Pour the mixture into your ice pop molds, leaving ¼-inch at the top to let the mixture expand when it freezes. Insert the ice pop sticks and freeze. (See page 22 for the complete procedure.)

LEMON & GINGER

This is a favorite choice for those who love contrasting sensations. Prepare for something intense, sweet, spicy—and mouth-puckering.

- 2¾-inch piece of fresh ginger, peeled and finely chopped or grated
- 3½ cups water
- scant 1 cup granulated sugar
- finely grated zest of 3 lemons
- 5 tablespoons freshly squeezed lemon juice (from about 3 lemons)
- 8–10 extra-thin lemon slices (optional)

Put the ginger, water, sugar, and lemon zest in a small saucepan and bring to a simmer. Simmer until the sugar has dissolved, then remove the pan from the heat and let the syrup cool to room temperature.

Pour the mixture through a fine strainer, pressing down hard on the pieces of ginger with the back of a spoon to extract all the juices. Mix in the lemon juice.

Pour the mixture into your ice pop molds, leaving ¼-inch at the top to let the mixture expand when it freezes. Place a slice of lemon, if using, into each mold, then insert an ice pop stick and freeze. (See page 22 for the complete procedure.)

BLACKBERRY

When my daughter Lily and I stay with my mother over the summer, we test the blackberries on the roadside outside her house until they're just sweet enough and then we have fun turning these into dark purple-striped ice pops by mixing in a touch of cream or yogurt. They look like Rothko paintings.

- 3½ cups blackberries
- ⅔ cup granulated sugar
- 3 teaspoons freshly squeezed lime or lemon juice
- 1¾ cups water
- 6 tablespoons heavy cream or Greek yogurt (optional)

Put the blackberries, sugar, lime, or lemon juice and water in a food processor and blend gradually to a puree.

Pour the mixture into a fine strainer, stir it through, and press down on the solids with the back of a spoon to extract all the liquid.

If you want to make stripes, divide the blackberry mixture in half. Add the cream to one half and mix it in well. Pour enough pure blackberry mixture into each ice pop mold to reach about one-quarter of the way up. (See page 19 for more help on creating stripes.)

Freeze until slightly firm, about 1 hour, then pour the cream mixture on top. Freeze for another hour, then top with the remaining pure blackberry mixture. Insert an ice pop stick when all the layers are in. They should stay upright due to the half-frozen first layers. Freeze completely. (See page 22 for the complete procedure.)

STRAWBERRIES & CREAM

This English classic is wonderful as it is, but look how it can be transformed with the inspired variations below.

- ½ cup plus 2 tablespoons granulated sugar
- ½ cup water
- 3 cups strawberries, rinsed, hulled, and cut in half
- 2 tablespoons freshly squeezed lemon juice
- 8 teaspoons heavy cream

Put the ½ cup sugar and the water in a small saucepan and bring to a simmer. Simmer until the sugar has dissolved.

Put the strawberries, sugar syrup, and lemon juice in a food processor and blend to a puree.

Stir the 2 tablespoons sugar into the cream. Divide the cream between your ice pop molds (about 1 tablespoon cream each), then pour the strawberry mixture on top. Insert the ice pop sticks and freeze. (See page 22 for the complete procedure.)

Variations:
Turn this into a French classic by adding 5 tablespoons red wine to the strawberries.

For an Italian spin add 2 tablespoons balsamic vinegar, a pinch of black ground pepper, and 2 tablespoons finely chopped fresh basil to the mix.

For an exotic touch, add 1 tablespoon rosewater to the cream. I like to add 5 tablespoons sweet sherry to the strawberries.

TART PLUM

There are endless varieties of plum and they all work beautifully in an ice pop. It's the skins that give the most flavor and that turn a plum into a tart plum when poached. Apparently there are more plum varieties in the world than there are of any other fruit. The promiscuous plum!

- 1½ pounds plums, rinsed, quartered, and pitted
- 1½ cups water
- ½-scant ⅔ cup granulated sugar (depending on the sweetness of the plums)
- 4 tablespoons freshly squeezed lemon juice
- 4 tablespoons elderflower cordial (optional)

Put the plums, water, sugar, and lemon juice in a saucepan and bring to a simmer. Simmer for 10 to 15 minutes until the plums break down. Remove the pan from the heat and let the mixture cool for a few minutes. Transfer the mixture to a food processor and add the elderflower cordial, if using. Blend, making sure you allow some small chunks to remain.

Pour the mixture into your ice pop molds, leaving ¼-inch at the top to let the mixture expand when it freezes. You can create a stripe with 2 different types of plum—see page 19. Insert the ice pop sticks and freeze. (See page 22 for the complete procedure.)

Variations:
Greengage plums are one of our favorites and pairs well with elderflower—add 4 tablespoons elderflower cordial. Plums also pair well with almond—add 1 teaspoon almond extract. A tablespoon of freshly grated ginger can also add a nice kick.

CANTALOUPE & BASIL

Choose a sweetly fragrant Cantaloupe melon that seems heavy for its size. It's great with just lemon or lime in an ice pop, but adding fresh basil adds complexity of flavor.

- ¾ cup water
- ¼ cup plus 2 tablespoons granulated sugar
- 15 fresh basil leaves (optional)
- 1¼ pounds cantaloupe melon chunks (from about 1 small melon)
- 4 tablespoons freshly squeezed lime or lemon juice

Put the water, sugar, and basil, if using, in a small saucepan and bring to a simmer. Simmer until the sugar has dissolved.

Remove the pan from the heat and let the mixture cool to room temperature. Pick out the basil leaves, squeezing any juice back into the pan.

Put the cantaloupe chunks in a food processor and blend to a smooth puree. Add the basil syrup and lime or lemon juice and blend again.

Pour the mixture into your ice pop molds, leaving ¼-inch at the top to let the mixture expand when it freezes. Insert the ice pop sticks and freeze. (See page 22 for the complete procedure.)

Variations:
Try using fresh mint or tarragon instead of basil.

Cantaloupe and honeydew melons pair well with fresh ginger—add 2 tablespoons freshly grated ginger to the syrup.

Melon is also nice with port—add 3-4 tablespoons to the food processor.

LYCHEE & LEMONGRASS

This recipe requires a little work, but if you love lychees then it becomes a labor of love. It's always better to use fresh fruit, but in this case you could also use canned lychee. This ice pop has a very special, delicate, and distinctive flavor, in which both the lychee and lemongrass shine through.

- 2 lemongrass stalks
- 1½ cups water
- ¼ cup plus 2 tablespoons granulated sugar
- finely grated zest of 1 lime
- 1 pound 2 ounces lychees (22–25 lychees), peeled and pitted
- 2–3 tablespoons freshly squeezed lime juice

Slice the lemongrass stalks into ¼-inch pieces and put them in a small saucepan with the water, sugar, and lime zest. Bring to a simmer and simmer for 3 minutes to extract the lemongrass aroma.

Remove the pan from the heat and let the syrup steep for at least 10 minutes. Pour the syrup through a fine strainer, pressing down hard on the pieces of lemongrass and lime zest to extract the juices.

Put the lychee flesh in a food processor and blend until smooth. Add the lemongrass syrup and blend again. Strain the mixture again, into a bowl, and stir in the lime juice.

Pour the mixture into your ice pop molds, leaving ¼-inch at the top to let the mixture expand when it freezes. Insert the ice pop sticks and freeze. (See page 22 for the complete procedure.)

DRENCHED WATERMELON

If you're wondering why this ice pop's called "drenched," it's because we suggest squeezing lime juice over it as you eat it. Out of curiosity one morning, I started dipping this ice pop into white rum—it was so good that I couldn't stop! Try it—just make sure you do it in the evening rather than the morning!

- 4 tablespoons water
- scant ⅓ cup granulated sugar
- 1½ pounds watermelon, seeded and cut into chunks
- 5 tablespoons freshly squeezed lime juice
- a pinch of salt
- 2 limes, cut into wedges to squeeze on the ice pops as you eat them

Put the water and sugar in a small saucepan and bring to a simmer. Simmer until the sugar has dissolved.

Remove the pan from the heat and let the syrup cool for a few minutes. Meanwhile, put the watermelon in a food processor and blend until smooth. Add the lime juice, salt, and sugar syrup and blend again. If there are any seeds, strain the mixture through a fine strainer.

Pour the mixture into your ice pop molds, leaving ¼-inch at the top to let the mixture expand when it freezes. Insert the ice pop sticks and freeze. (See page 22 for the complete procedure.)

Squeeze fresh lime juice on the frozen ice pop as you eat it and also dip it in white rum if you like.

Variation:
Throw a handful of torn mint leaves into the sugar syrup as it heats. When cooled, squeeze the leaves with your fingers before discarding.

STRAWBERRY & PEPPER

The bite of black pepper in a fruit ice pop is very interesting, but wearing a cap of white chocolate is truly inspired. Good going Cesar, and it looks artistic too!

- ¼ cup granulated sugar
- 3 tablespoons water
- 3 cups strawberries, rinsed, hulled, and cut in half
- a squeeze of lemon juice
- 30 black peppercorns, finely ground or smashed

Put the sugar and water in a small saucepan over medium heat and bring to a simmer. Simmer until the sugar has dissolved.

Put the strawberries in a food processor and blend to a puree. Add the sugar syrup, lemon juice, and pepper and blend again.

Pour the mixture into your ice pop molds, leaving ¼-inch at the top to let the mixture expand when it freezes. Insert the ice pop sticks and freeze. (See page 22 for the complete procedure.)

This is great on its own, but to give it a white chocolate cap, follow the instructions on page 20.

PEACHES & CREAM

Choose peaches that are fragrant and firm with a little give; they are at their best at the height of summer. Poaching them intensifies their flavor.

- 1 pound 10 ounces peaches (about 4 large or 8 small peaches)
- generous 1 cup water
- ½ cup granulated sugar
- freshly squeezed juice of 1 lemon
- 1 teaspoon vanilla extract (optional)
- 5 tablespoons heavy cream

Plunge the peaches in boiling water and leave for 2 minutes. The skins will come loose, so you should be able to peel them off easily.

Pit the peaches and cut them into chunks. Put the water, sugar, and lemon juice in a wide saucepan and bring to a simmer. Simmer until the sugar has dissolved, then add the peach chunks. Simmer for an additonal 5 minutes, or until the peaches are tender. Remove the pan from the heat and let cool to room temperature.

Put the peaches, syrup, and vanilla, if using, in a food processor and blend to a puree. Mix in the cream, or pour 1 teaspoon cream into each ice pop mold. Pour the mixture into the molds, leaving ¼ inch at the top to let the mixture expand when it freezes. Insert the ice pop sticks and freeze. (See page 22 for the complete procedure.)

Variation:
To make peach Bellini ice pops, leave out the cream and add scant ½ cup Prosecco to the mix, or just dip the ice pop into Prosecco as you eat it.

BLUEBERRY & YOGURT

Now that blueberries are abundant, their popularity has soared. This is great because the health benefits and flavor are utterly delightful, especially when teamed with their old friend yogurt.

- 2 cups blueberries
- 7 tablespoons water
- ¼ cup plus 2 tablespoons granulated sugar
- generous 2 cups Greek yogurt
- 8 tablespoons honey
- 3 tablespoons freshly squeezed lemon juice

Put the blueberries, 5 tablespoons water, and sugar in a saucepan and bring to a simmer. Simmer over low heat for 3 to 5 minutes until the blueberries burst. Remove the pan from the heat and set aside.

Mix together the yogurt, honey, lemon juice, and the 2 tablespoons water in a bowl.

Spoon alternate layers of the yogurt and blueberry mixtures into each ice pop mold, leaving ¼-inch at the top to let the mixture expand when it freezes. Insert the ice pop sticks and freeze. (See page 22 for the complete procedure.)

APRICOT & PISTACHIO

Apricots make deliciously velvety ice pops. Make them in mid-summer before the apricots vanish for the year again. Choose ones that are only very slightly soft and have a sweet aroma, as those are the tastiest. This combination has a Middle Eastern charm.

- 1 2/3 cups water
- 2/3 cup granulated sugar
- 2 tablespoons freshly squeezed lemon juice
- 1 pound 2 ounces apricots, cut in half and pitted
- 1/2 teaspoon almond extract
- 1/4 cup shelled pistachios, chopped

Put the water, sugar, and lemon juice in a medium saucepan and bring to a simmer. Simmer until the sugar has dissolved.

Add the apricots and simmer until they have broken down—about 5 to 10 minutes. Remove the pan from the heat and let the mixture cool to room temperature.

Stir in the almond extract and chopped pistachios until well mixed.

Pour the mixture into your ice pop molds, leaving 1/4-inch at the top to let the mixture expand when it freezes. Insert the ice pop sticks and freeze. (See page 22 for the complete procedure.)

It's nice to roll the ice pops in pistachios before serving, too (see page 20).

Variation:
You can add 3/4 cup heavy cream to the apricots after they're cooked, and only use scant 1 cup water.

PEACH & TARRAGON

Cesar likes to roast the peaches for these ice pops, since it gives them a slightly caramelized quality. There's no need to peel the peaches because their skins add to the texture and depth to this recipe, which also works well with nectarines, apricots, or plums.

- scant 1 cup water
- ½ cup granulated sugar
- leaves from 6 fresh leafy tarragon sprigs
- 1 pound 10 ounces peaches (4 large or 8 small peaches), cut in half
- 2 tablespoons freshly squeezed lemon juice
- 2 teaspoons vanilla extract

Preheat the oven to 350°F.

Put the water, sugar, and tarragon leaves in a small saucepan and bring to a simmer. Simmer until the sugar has dissolved. Remove the pan from the heat and let the mixture cool while you roast the peaches.

Place the peaches on a cookie sheet. Bake them in the preheated oven for about 30 minutes until they are tender. Take them out of the oven and set them aside until they are cool enough to handle.

Pit the peaches and put the flesh, tarragon syrup, lemon juice, and vanilla in a food processor. Blend to a puree.

Pour the mixture into your ice pop molds, leaving ¼-inch at the top to let the mixture expand when it freezes. Insert the ice pop sticks and freeze. (See page 22 for the complete procedure.)

RUBY GRAPEFRUIT & CAMPARI

This was the first ice pop we ever made. It became a signature flavor along the High Line in New York and has remained a favorite in London at the South Bank.

- ½ cup water
- ½ cup granulated sugar
- 2½ cups fresh ruby red grapefruit juice (from about 4 grapefruits)
- ⅓ cup Campari

Put the water and sugar in a small saucepan and bring to a simmer. Simmer until the sugar has dissolved. Mix together with the grapefruit juice and Campari.

Pour the mixture into your ice pop molds, leaving ¼-inch at the top to let the mixture expand when it freezes. Insert the ice pop sticks and freeze. (See page 22 for the complete procedure.)

SWEET PEAR & GINGER

Pear and ginger are a classic pairing. You can use any variety of pear here, like Bosc, Williams, Anjou, or Forelle. We often use Comice. For extra indulgence, try melting a little dark chocolate and drizzling it into the pear mixture.

- scant 1 cup water
- ½-scant ⅔ cup granulated sugar (depending on the sweetness of the pears)
- 2 ¾-inch piece of fresh ginger, peeled and finely chopped or grated
- 2 pounds pears (3-4 pears)
- 3 tablespoons freshly squeezed lemon juice
- ⅔ cup heavy cream or crème fraîche (optional)

Put the water, sugar, and ginger in a wide saucepan and bring to a simmer. Simmer for 3 minutes, then remove the pan from the heat and let the syrup cool for a few minutes.

Pour the syrup through a fine strainer, pressing down hard on the pieces of ginger with the back of a spoon to extract all the juices. We leave some ginger pieces in for a stronger ginger taste.

Peel, core, and chop the pears, then put them immediately in the syrup so that they don't turn brown. Cover the pan and simmer until tender—about 10 minutes. Remove the pan from the heat and add the lemon juice. Let the pears and syrup cool for a few minutes. Put the cooled pears and syrup in a food processor and lightly blend to a puree. Stir in the cream or crème fraîche, if using.

Pour the mixture into your ice pop molds, leaving ¼-inch at the top to let the mixture expand when it freezes. Insert the ice pop sticks and freeze. (See page 22 for the complete procedure.)

CHERRY & RED CURRANT

The characteristics of cherry and red currant combine for a sweet and tart treat in this pretty ice pop. It requires a little patience to create the stripes, but it's fun for kids and for the young at heart.

For the cherry stripe:
- 1¾ cups water
- scant ⅔–¾ cup granulated sugar
- 1 pound 2 ounces cherries
- 4 tablespoons freshly squeezed lemon juice
- ¼ teaspoon almond extract (optional)

For the red currant stripe:
- 1⅓ cups red currants
- 1¼ cups water
- scant ⅓ cup granulated sugar

For the cherry stripe, put the water and sugar in a saucepan and bring to a simmer. Simmer until the sugar has dissolved. Add the cherries and simmer for 20 minutes, covered with a lid. Pour the cherries and syrup through a fine strainer, stirring hard and pressing down on the cherries with the back of a spoon to extract all the juices. Discard the cherry pits and skins. Stir in the lemon juice and almond extract, if using.

For the red currant stripe, put the red currants, water, and sugar in a saucepan and bring to a simmer. Simmer for 5 minutes, or until the currants burst. Put the mixture in a food processor and blend to a puree. Strain through a fine strainer, stirring well and pressing down hard on the solids with the back of a spoon to extract all the juices.

To create the stripes, freeze alternate layers of cherry and red currant in your ice pop molds. Freeze each layer for about 1 hour, leaving ¼-inch at the top of the mold after the last layer to let the mixture expand when it freezes. Insert the ice pop sticks when all the layers are in. They should stay upright due to the half-frozen first layers. Freeze completely. (See page 22 for the complete procedure.)

FRESH MANGO

Cesar dedicates this to Meekal, one of his favorite customers down at the South Bank market in London. He often bought 2 ice pops for each of his 3 kids and we had to promise him we'd hold reserves over the winter. The key to this recipe is finding the juiciest, ripest, and most flavorful mangoes. There are so many Pakistani and Indian varieties, each with their own sweet, unique character. We love Pakistani honey mangoes, and Indian Alphonso and Kesar mangoes.

- 4-5 medium Indian or Pakistani mangoes, or 3-4 larger Brazilian or other mangoes
- a squeeze of lemon juice
- generous 1 cup water

Peel the mangoes and carefully cut the flesh away from the central seed, facing the knife away from yourself.

Put the mango flesh in a processor and blend—you should get about 2¼ cups smooth mango pulp.

Add a tiny squeeze of lemon juice. You should barely be able to taste the lemon at this point—it should just lift the amazing mango flavor. Add the water and blend again.

Pour the mixture into your ice pop molds, leaving ¼-inch at the top to let the mixture expand when it freezes. Insert the ice pop sticks and freeze. (See page 22 for the complete procedure.)

Make sure you make enough to last until next year!

CLEMENTINE, WHITE WINE & ROSE

A man in a Spanish wine store suggested this combination from a drink he remembered, and it turned out beautifully. Make this light, elegant ice pop using the Spanish white wine Verdejo—zesty, with tropical notes—or substitute another dry white wine. The optional basil leaves add a complexity to the flavor.

8–10

- finely grated zest of 2 clementines
- 5 tablespoons water
- ½ cup granulated sugar
- small handful of fresh basil leaves (optional)
- ½ cup white wine (Verdejo is best)
- 2¼ cups freshly squeezed clementine juice (from about 12 clementines)
- 3 tablespoons freshly squeezed lemon juice
- 1 tablespoon rosewater

Put the clementine zest, water, sugar, and basil leaves, if using, in a small saucepan and bring to a simmer. Simmer until the sugar has dissolved. Remove the pan from the heat and let the mixture cool to room temperature.

Pick out the basil leaves, squeezing any juice back into the pan. Pour the wine, clementine, and lemon juices, and rosewater into the sugar syrup and mix well.

Pour the mixture into your ice pop molds, leaving ¼-inch at the top to let the mixture expand when it freezes. Insert the ice pop sticks and freeze. (See page 22 for the complete procedure.)

PINEAPPLE & COCONUT

This child-friendly combination is an escape to the sun. We love the sweet acidity of the pineapple with the mellow coconut. Adults can dip this in rum or sprinkle coconut flakes on top, or they can add rum to the mixture to turn it into a Piña Colada. Choose a plump pineapple with a sweet scent and healthy green leaves.

- 1 pineapple
- freshly squeezed juice and finely grated zest of 1 lemon
- $2/3$ cup granulated sugar
- $1 3/4$ cups unsweetened coconut milk
- 4 tablespoons rum (optional)

Cut the crown off the pineapple and discard. Cut the pineapple in half lengthwise, cut away the peel with a sharp knife, and cut out any remaining "eyes." Cut each half in half again, lengthwise. Cut away and discard the hard core, then cube the flesh.

Put the pineapple cubes, lemon juice and zest, sugar, and coconut milk in a food processor and blend, allowing some chunks to remain. Taste and add more sugar, if needed. If you decide to add rum, stir it in now.

Pour the mixture into your ice pop molds, leaving $1/4$-inch at the top to let the mixture expand when it freezes. Insert the ice pop sticks and freeze. (See page 22 for the complete procedure.)

Variation:
For a sharper, very lively-tasting ice pop, replace the coconut milk with $1 2/3$ cups fresh orange juice or water and dip the frozen ice pop in coconut flakes, if you like.

COCONUT & LIME

You know the song—now here's the ice pop! (If you don't know the Harry Nilsson song, "Coconut" in which he sings about putting the lime in the coconut, give it a play and enjoy yourself!) The ice pop is tangy, creamy, and so easy to make, and it really benefits from being made with good-quality coconut milk.

- 1¾ cups unsweetened coconut milk
- finely grated zest of 2 limes
- ⅔ cup freshly squeezed lime juice (from about 4-5 limes)
- 1¾ cups sweetened condensed milk
- a good pinch of salt

Put all the ingredients into a large bowl and mix with a spoon until fully blended.

Pour the mixture into your ice pop molds, leaving ¼-inch at the top to let the mixture expand when it freezes. Insert the ice pop sticks and freeze. (See page 22 for the complete procedure.)

When ready to eat, it's nice to dip the ice pop in toasted dry unsweetened coconut. Or splash it with rum!

BANANA CHOCODIP

Monkey around with this ice pop that children love. You can add a couple of spoons of Nutella, peanut butter, or oat bran to the mix if you desire—it's all good! The banana flavor mysteriously intensifies the longer the ice pops stay frozen.

- 3 medium bananas
- 1 teaspoon freshly squeezed lemon juice
- ⅔ cup heavy cream
- ¾ cup whole milk
- ½ teaspoon vanilla extract
- 4 tablespoons maple syrup or honey
- 3½ ounces milk or dark chocolate
- 1 tablespoon vegetable oil

Put the bananas, lemon juice, cream, milk, vanilla, and maple syrup or honey in a food processor and blend until smooth.

Pour the mixture into your ice pop molds, leaving ¼-inch at the top to let the mixture expand when it freezes. Insert the ice pop sticks and freeze. (See page 22 for the complete procedure.)

To cap the frozen ice pops with chocolate, see page 20.

CRANBERRY & ORANGE

This is the perfect way to end a rich Christmas dinner: deck the halls with this festive ice pop! If you're sitting around the table, try dipping the ice pop into a bowl of orange liqueur or vodka.

- 2¼ cups water
- generous ¾ cup plus 2 tablespoons granulated sugar
- 2 cups cranberries
- scant 1 cup freshly squeezed orange juice (from about 2 oranges)
- freshly squeezed juice of 1 lemon
- scant ½ cup heavy cream or crème fraîche

Put the water and the generous ¾ cup sugar in a medium saucepan and bring to a simmer. Simmer until the sugar has dissolved. Drop in the cranberries and simmer for an additonal 6 minutes, or until the berries have burst and the juices are released.

Remove the pan from the heat and let cool to room temperature.

Put the mixture in a food processor and blend to a puree. Pour the mixture through a fine strainer, pressing with the back of a spoon to extract all the juices. Stir in the orange and lemon juices.

Stir the 2 tablespoons sugar into the cream. Divide the cranberry mixture in half and stir the cream into one half. Mix lightly. Divide the cranberry cream between your ice pop molds. (See page 19 for more help on creating stripes.)

Freeze until slightly firm, about 1 hour, then pour the pure cranberry mixture on top. Insert the ice pop sticks and freeze completely. (See page 22 for the complete procedure.)

RHUBARB & CUSTARD

This very tangy creamy English classic is satisfaction immortalized in ice.

For the rhubarb:
- 1¼ cups water
- ½ cup granulated sugar
- 14 ounces rhubarb, trimmed and roughly chopped

For the custard:
- 1¾ cups whole milk
- scant 1 cup heavy cream
- 4 egg yolks
- ⅔ cup granulated sugar
- 2 teaspoons vanilla extract
- a pinch of salt

For the rhubarb, put the water and sugar in a medium saucepan and bring to a simmer. Simmer until the sugar has dissolved. Add the rhubarb and simmer for an additional 10 minutes, or until the rhubarb has broken down. Remove the pan from the heat.

For the custard, pour the milk and cream in a saucepan over low heat. Beat the egg yolks and sugar together in a heatproof bowl. When the milk starts to simmer, take it off the heat and spoon a few ladles of it into the egg mixture. Whisk it well, then pour it back into the pan. Heat up the mixture again over low-medium heat, stirring constantly, until it has thickened enough to easily coat the back of a wooden spoon. Do not let it boil. Pour it immediately into a bowl, stir in the vanilla and salt, and let it cool down before refrigerating it for a couple of hours or overnight to thicken.

Spoon alternate layers of rhubarb and custard into your ice pop molds, leaving ¼-inch at the top to let the mixture expand when it freezes. Insert the ice pop sticks and freeze. (See page 22 for the complete procedure.)

WHITE GRAPEFRUIT & STAR ANISE

Star anise is the fruit of a 25-foot Chinese evergreen magnolia tree. Its subtle licorice aroma shines through the sharpness of the grapefruit. Make sure you use yellow-skinned ("white") grapefruit, and steep the star anise for as long as possible in the sugar syrup. (We steep it overnight.) For an extra spike, you can dip this ice pop in a glass of anise-flavored liqueur, such as Pernod, Pastis, ouzo, or arak. It makes an exciting predinner treat.

8–10

- ½ cup water
- scant ⅔ cup granulated sugar
- grated zest of 1 white grapefruit
- 4–6 whole star anise
- 2½ cups freshly squeezed white grapefruit juice (from about 4–5 grapefruits)

Put the water, sugar, grapefruit zest, and star anise in a saucepan and bring to a simmer. Simmer for 5 minutes. Remove the pan from the heat and let the star anise infuse at least until the syrup has cooled to room temperature, but preferably overnight.

Pull out the star anise from the mixture, but it does look beautiful if you then drop one inside the ice pop mold before filling. Add the grapefruit juice to the syrup and stir. Pour the mixture into your ice pop molds, leaving ¼-inch at the top to let the mixture expand when it freezes. Insert the ice pop sticks and freeze. (See page 22 for the complete procedure.)

EGYPTIAN HIBISCUS & PEACH

The ancient Egyptian hibiscus drink called "karkadé" inspired this sweet and tart, ruby-colored ice pop. It is very popular in Egypt, where our family came from, and in the Sudan, where my grandparents and Cesar's great grandparents once lived. You can find dried hibiscus in most Middle Eastern stores.

- 1½ ounces dried hibiscus, briefly rinsed in cold water
- 3¾ cups water
- ½ cup plus 4 tablespoons granulated sugar
- 2 peaches, pitted and cut into slim wedges

Put the hibiscus and water in a saucepan, bring to a boil, and simmer for 5 minutes. Remove the pan from the heat and stir in ½ cup plus 2 tablespoons sugar. Let the mixture steep for a few hours.

Strain the mixture through a fine strainer, pressing on the hibiscus with the back of a spoon to extract the liquid, or squeeze it with your hands. Put the peaches in a small bowl, sprinkle with the remaining 2 tablespoons of sugar, and let them macerate for 30 minutes. Put a few macerated peach slices and their juices into each ice pop mold, then pour the hibiscus mixture in, leaving ¼ inch at the top to let the mixture expand when it freezes. Insert the ice pop sticks and freeze. (See page 22 for the complete procedure.)

Variations:
Mix 1 teaspoon orange blossom or rosewater, or 1 teaspoon freshly grated ginger into the hibiscus water after you take it off the heat, or mix it into the peaches.

BURGUNDY BERRY

This mix of berries and wine is great to serve after dinner or at a garden party. Be careful not to let your hand slip, as too much alcohol will result in a slushy ice pop. Pour a little cream at the bottom of each mold for something extra sublime.

- 1¾ cups fresh berries, e.g. raspberries, blackberries, blueberries, plus an extra scant 1¼ cups blackberries
- ¾ cup granulated sugar
- 2 teaspoons freshly squeezed lemon juice
- ½ cup Burgundy (or red wine of your choice)
- ½ cup water
- scant ½ cup heavy cream (optional)

Put the 1¾ cups fresh berries in a bowl, stir in scant ½ cup of the sugar, and the lemon juice, and set aside to macerate for at least 1 hour until the juices are released.

Meanwhile, put the wine, water, the scant 1¼ cups blackberries, and remaining sugar in a food processor and gently blend. Pour the mixture through a fine strainer, stirring with a spoon and pressing down to extract all the juices.

If using the cream, drizzle a teaspoon into each ice pop mold, then loosely press the macerated berries into each mold and pour the wine mixture over them, leaving ¼-inch at the top to let the mixture expand when it freezes. Insert the ice pop sticks and freeze. (See page 22 for the complete procedure.)

MOJITO

We created this ice pop for an outdoor summer wedding party near London. It's Cesar's favorite cocktail and we were determined to develop it into an ice pop. It's since become a top-seller from the cart for people to wind down in the evening along the South Bank of the river. If you put too much rum in this it will turn mushy, so if you want more, dip the frozen ice pop in rum as you eat it.

- 2¼ cups water
- generous ¾ cup granulated sugar
- 1 cup fresh mint leaves plus 20 extra leaves
- scant 1 cup freshly squeezed lime juice (from about 5-6 limes)
- 4 tablespoons white rum
- 10 extra thin lime slices to suspend in the molds

Put the water and sugar in a small saucepan and bring to a boil. Remove the pan from the heat and drop in the 1 cup of mint leaves. Cover with a lid, refrigerate, and steep for a few hours or overnight.

Strain the syrup through a fine strainer, squeezing any juice from the mint leaves back into the pan. Finely chop 10 of the 20 extra mint leaves and add them to the syrup with the lime juice and rum and mix well. It should taste quite sharp.

Drop a slice of lime into each ice pop mold along with a mint leaf. Ladle in the mixture, leaving ¼-inch at the top to let the mixture expand when it freezes. Insert the ice pop sticks (the lime slices will be pushed down again to the bottom by the sticks) and freeze. (See page 22 for the complete procedure.)

SWEET SHERRY & RAISIN

This treasure of an ice pop is so good—please try it! I made it for my mother's Spanish book launch party, as it's inspired by the famous Malaga ice cream. The poet laureate Mark Strand was there and said it was the best dessert he'd ever tasted—poetry to my ears!

- ¼ cup small black raisins or currants
- ¼ cup Pedro Ximénez sherry (thick, dark, and aged)
- 1½ cups heavy cream
- generous 1 cup whole milk
- ¼ cup granulated sugar
- 1 small cinnamon stick
- 5 egg yolks
- 1 teaspoon vanilla extract

Put the raisins or currants and sherry in a bowl and let soak. Put the cream, milk, sugar, and cinnamon stick in a small saucepan and heat until almost boiling. Remove the pan from the heat.

In a medium bowl, briefly whisk the egg yolks, then gradually add a ladleful of the hot milk, then another, whisking constantly. Pour this back into the pan. Heat up the mixture again over low heat, stirring constantly, until it has thickened enough to easily coat the back of a wooden spoon. Do not let it boil. Strain it immediately through a fine strainer into a bowl, stir in the vanilla, and let it cool before refrigerating it for 2 hours or overnight to thicken.

Add the raisin and sherry mixture to the cold custard and stir gently. Pour the mixture into your ice pop molds, leaving ¼-inch at the top to let the mixture expand when it freezes. Insert the ice pop sticks and freeze. (See page 22 for the complete procedure.) If you like, sprinkle on a small pinch of cinnamon on the frozen pop.

ALMOND & ORANGE BLOSSOM

There's nothing like the wonderful, delicate taste of almonds and orange blossom blended together. For me, they conjure up childhood memories of Middle Eastern pastries. The ground almonds give a very nice texture to this ice pop.

- 2¼ cups whole milk
- scant ¼ cup cornstarch
- generous 1 cup heavy cream
- ½ cup plus 2 tablespoons granulated sugar
- 3 teaspoons orange blossom water
- 5 drops of almond extract
- scant ½ cup ground almonds
- handful of slivered almonds, to coat the ice pops

Put 3 tablespoons of the milk in a small bowl and mix in the cornstarch to form a smooth paste. Pour the remaining milk, the cream, and sugar in a medium saucepan and heat until just about to simmer, then stir in the cornstarch paste. Stir constantly until the mixture starts to thicken and bubble. Let thicken, stirring constantly, for an additional 2 minutes.

Pour the mixture through a fine strainer into a bowl. Stir in the orange blossom and almond extract and let cool to room temperature.

Stir the ground almonds into the mixture until blended. Pour the mixture into your ice pop molds, leaving ¼-inch at the top to let the mixture expand when it freezes. Insert the ice pop sticks and freeze. (See page 22 for the complete procedure.) When you are ready to enjoy the ice pops, roll them in slivered almonds (see page 20).

PISTACHIO & ROSE

I loved the Egyptian milk dessert called "muhallabeya" that my mother used to make for me as a child. She sprinkled it with pistachios and scented it with rosewater. Several years ago when she came to visit, she helped me recreate it in this ice pop.

- 2¼ cups whole milk
- scant ¼ cup cornstarch
- generous 1 cup heavy cream
- ½ cup plus 2 tablespoons granulated sugar
- 3 teaspoons rosewater (rosewaters vary in strength, so adjust to taste)
- ¼ cup shelled pistachios, finely chopped

Put 3 tablespoons of the milk in a small bowl and mix in the cornstarch to form a smooth paste. Pour the remaining milk, the cream, and sugar in a medium saucepan and heat until just about to simmer, then stir in the cornstarch paste. Stir constantly until the mixture starts to thicken and bubble. Let thicken, stirring constantly, for an additional 2 minutes.

Pour the mixture through a fine strainer into a bowl. Stir in the rosewater and let cool to room temperature.

Stir the pistachios into the mixture until well blended, reserving a few for coating the ice pops. Pour the mixture into your ice pop molds, leaving ¼-inch at the top to let the mixture expand when it freezes. Insert the ice pop sticks and freeze. (See page 22 for the complete procedure.)

When you are ready to enjoy the ice pops, roll them in more chopped pistachios (see page 20).

MINTED MILK

We had so many recipes in mind for this book, but after composing this one, we knew immediately that it had to be included. It's so addictive that Lily devoured every last one in the batch.

8–10

- 1½ cups fresh mint leaves (a large bunch of about 20 sprigs)
- 2 cups whole milk
- generous 1 cup heavy cream
- ½ cup plus 2 tablespoons granulated sugar

Crush the mint leaves a little with the back of a spoon: this will help to turn the milk pastel green.

Put the milk, cream, and sugar in a saucepan and bring almost to a boil. Remove the pan from the heat and add the mint leaves. Cover and let cool. The longer you can let the mint infuse the better. Strain the mixture through a fine strainer, pressing down on the leaves with the back of a spoon or squeezing them with your hands to extract the juices.

Pour the mixture into your ice pop molds, leaving ¼-inch at the top to let the mixture expand when it freezes. Insert the ice pop sticks and freeze. (See page 22 for the complete procedure.) If you like you can artfully drip some melted dark chocolate over the ice pop (see page 20 for help with melting chocolate).

Variation:
Turn this into a minted chocolate ice pop by warming the minted milk up again after you take out the mint leaves, then stirring in 2¼ ounces chopped dark chocolate. Let the mixture cool completely so that the chocolate is fully integrated.

THREE MILKS LEMON DESSERT

The famous Mexican "tres leches" cake, made with 3 kinds of milk or cream, is one of the best desserts ever invented. Here we've given it a spin for all lemon lovers. This one's easy!

- 1¾ cups sweetened condensed milk
- ⅔ cup whole milk
- ⅔ cup heavy cream
- generous 1 cup freshly squeezed lemon juice (from 3 lemons)
- finely grated zest of 2 lemons

Put all the ingredients together in a bowl and whisk until smooth and combined.

Pour the mixture into your ice pop molds, leaving ¼-inch at the top to let the mixture expand when it freezes. Insert the ice pop sticks and freeze. (See page 22 for the complete procedure.)

Variation:
If you like, you can crumble some pieces of cake or ladyfingers into the mix.

FRENCH TWIST

The marriage of French vanilla and raspberries works so well, which explains why this ice pop is so popular. The small amount of vodka keeps the raspberries from freezing solid.

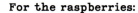

For the raspberries:
- scant 2½ cups raspberries (fresh or frozen)
- ½ cup granulated sugar
- 2 tablespoons vodka (optional)

For the French vanilla:
- 1¾ cups whole milk
- scant 1 cup heavy cream
- a pinch of salt
- 1 vanilla bean
- 4 egg yolks
- ⅔ cup granulated sugar

For the raspberries, put the raspberries in a bowl and pour the sugar and vodka over them. Set aside for at least 1 hour or overnight so the raspberries release their juices.

For the French vanilla, put the milk, cream, and salt in a saucepan over low heat. Cut along the vanilla bean and scrape the seeds out into the pan and add the bean too. Beat the egg yolks and sugar in a heatproof bowl. When the milk starts to simmer, take it off the heat and pour a few spoons of it into the egg mixture. Whisk well, then pour back into the pan. Heat over low-medium heat, stirring constantly, until thickened enough to easily coat the back of a wooden spoon. Do not let it boil. Strain it immediately through a fine strainer and let cool, then refrigerate for at least 2 hours.

Mash the raspberry mixture lightly, leaving some raspberries almost whole. Spoon alternate layers of the raspberries and French vanilla into your ice pop molds, leaving ¼-inch at the top to let the mixture expand when it freezes. Muddle the layers together a little with an ice pop stick. Insert the ice pop sticks and freeze. (See page 22 for the complete procedure.)

50s ORANGE CHEESECAKE

Here is a twist on our amazingly popular 50s orange ice pop, a real hit with New Yorkers. We've morphed it into a cheesecake! The orange oils from the zest are what gives this a special flavor. It's easy to make and uniquely delicious.

- finely grated zest of 3 oranges
- ¾ cup granulated sugar
- scant ½ cup cream cheese
- generous 1 cup sour cream
- 1⅔ cups freshly squeezed orange juice (from about 4 oranges)
- 2¼ ounces graham crackers (optional)

Put the orange zest and sugar in a food processor and blend for about 1 minute until the sugar is bright orange. Add the cream cheese and blend for a few more seconds. Add the sour cream and blend for another few seconds. Add the orange juice and blend again until fully combined.

Pour the mixture into your ice pop molds, leaving ¼-inch at the top to let the mixture expand when it freezes. Insert the ice pop sticks and freeze. (See page 22 for the complete procedure.)

If you like, grind the crackers up with a mortar and pestle and sprinkle on the frozen ice pops, or leave the ice pops to melt only slightly and lightly dip them in a bowl of crumbs just before eating.

MILK & HONEY

This is what an ice pop should be: simple and delicious. The taste of the honey really shines through when it's frozen with milk and cream and it all melts beautifully together as you eat it. It's interesting to experiment with different honeys, such as acacia, orange blossoms, or lavender.

- 8 tablespoons honey
- 1½ cups whole milk
- 1½ cups heavy cream

Put the honey and 6 tablespoons of the milk in a small saucepan and heat until melted and well blended. Remove the pan from the heat and pour the mixture into a bowl with the cream and remaining milk, stirring until well blended.

Pour the mixture into your ice pop molds, leaving ¼-inch at the top to let the mixture expand when it freezes. Insert the ice pop sticks and freeze. (See page 22 for the complete procedure.)

CASSATA

We've managed to put Italy on a stick here, with this traditional Sicilian dessert converted to an ice pop. Creamy ricotta is mixed with chopped nuts like almonds and pistachios, chopped candied fruits, and tiny pieces of chocolate.

- 2 cups ricotta
- 1¾ cups heavy cream
- scant ¾ cup superfine sugar
- 2½ teaspoons vanilla extract
- 4-6 tablespoons milk, depending on the thickness of the ricotta
- 1 ounce candied orange peel
- 1 ounce candied lemon peel
- scant ¼ cup shelled pistachios
- scant ¼ cup blanched almonds
- 1½ ounces dark chocolate
- 1 teaspoon grated orange or lemon zest (optional)

Put the ricotta, cream, sugar, and vanilla in a food processor and blend very briefly until smooth. (The mix will thicken slightly.) Pour into a bowl and stir in the milk to thin the mixture, but not too much, as the chopped ingredients need to float in the mixture.

Chop the candied peels, nuts, and chocolate into small pieces and stir into the ricotta mixture. Mix in the zest, if using.

Spoon the mixture into your ice pop molds, and bang the molds hard on the table so there are no big air bubbles. Leave ¼-inch at the top to let the mixture expand when it freezes. Insert the ice pop sticks and freeze. (See page 22 for the complete procedure.) If you like, save a little chopped chocolate or candied fruit to sprinkle onto the frozen ice pops.

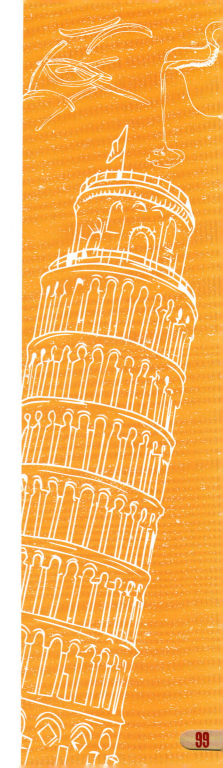

BUTTERSCOTCH

Smooth, silky, and comforting, butterscotch is irresistible to both children and adults.

- ½ cup granulated sugar
- 2 tablespoons unsalted butter
- generous 1 cup heavy cream
- 2¾ cups whole milk
- 1 teaspoon vanilla extract
- ¼ teaspoon salt

Put the sugar, butter, and cream in a saucepan and bring to a simmer over low heat. Simmer for about 10 to 12 minutes, stirring occasionally. Keep an eye on it and stir particularly toward the end as the mixture darkens to a dark amber and thickens: this is when the lovely butterscotch flavor develops.

Once it has turned dark amber, stir in the milk and bring back up to a simmer, then simmer for 2 minutes. Remove the pan from the heat, stir in the vanilla and salt, and let cool to room temperature.

Pour the mixture into your ice pop molds, leaving ¼-inch at the top to let the mixture expand when it freezes. Insert the ice pop sticks and freeze. (See page 22 for the complete procedure.)

Variation:
Bourbon is a good match with butterscotch. If you like, add 2-3 tablespoons to the mix at the end.

SONI'S KULFI

Our friend, Soni Bhatia, a talented chef who trained in Paris and ran the renowned Soni's supper club in San Francisco, insisted that we include a kulfi (Indian ice cream) ice pop in this book. This is her family recipe and together, we reconstructed it as an ice pop. The ground almonds give it a bite, but beware: these ice pops are rich, so we suggest using smallish molds.

- 5¼ cups whole milk
- 2 pinches of saffron threads
- 8 cardamom pods, crushed with a mortar and pestle
- ½ cup granulated sugar
- 1¼ cups heavy cream
- ⅔ cup ground almonds
- 4–5 drops of kewra extract (optional)
- scant ¼ cup shelled pistachios, chopped

Put the milk, saffron, and cardamom in a wide, heavy saucepan and bring to a boil. Leave a metal whisk in the saucepan to prevent the milk from boiling over. Simmer, and stir every 5 minutes or so, whisking back into the milk any skin that forms. Simmer until the milk has reduced to a third of the volume, about 35 minutes. There will be a slight caramel smell. Remove the pan from the heat and add the sugar, stirring until it has dissolved. Pour the mixture into another bowl to cool, then cover and refrigerate it for several hours to let the flavors blend.

Strain the mixture, stirring it through a strainer, then stir in the cream, ground almonds, and kewra extract, if using.

Pour the mixture into your ice pop molds, leaving ¼-inch at the top to let the mixture expand when it freezes. Sprinkle the chopped pistachios over the top. Insert the ice pop sticks and freeze. (See page 22 for the complete procedure.)

CEREAL MILK

Inspired by the famous cereal-milk soft serve that created a frenzy in New York City, we've created our own version by freezing Lily's morning cereal onto a stick and it was quite a hit! You can experiment with your favorite cereal. We know you'll agree it will taste even better in this frozen form.

- 1¼ cups whole milk
- generous 1 cup heavy cream
- 1 cup your favorite breakfast cereal (we like Cheerios), plus extra to drop into the molds
- 1 ripe banana, cut into ¾-inch slices
- 5-6 tablespoons honey or maple syrup

Mix all the ingredients together in a bowl, cover, and refrigerate overnight to let the liquid take on that unmistakably delicious cereal taste.

The next day, put the steeped mixture in a food processor and blend until smooth.

Pour the mixture into your ice pop molds, and drop in some extra pieces of cereal. Leave ¼-inch at the top to let the mixture expand when it freezes. Insert the ice pop sticks and freeze. (See page 22 for the complete procedure.)

NEW YORK BLACK & WHITE

We make this vanilla ice pop into the "New York Black & White" by dipping half of it in dark chocolate, and half in white, in homage to the much loved New York black and white cookie. You can tell how good an ice-cream chef is by how good their vanilla ice cream tastes.

8–10

For the vanilla:
- 1¾ cups whole milk
- scant 1 cup heavy cream
- ½ cup granulated sugar
- a pinch of salt
- 1 vanilla bean
- 4 egg yolks

For the dipping chocolate:
- 3½ ounces white chocolate
- 3½ ounces dark chocolate
- 2 tablespoons vegetable oil

Put the milk, cream, sugar, and salt in a saucepan over low heat. Cut along the vanilla bean and scrape the seeds out into the pan and add the bean too. Put the egg yolks in a heatproof bowl and briefly whisk. When the milk starts to simmer, take it off the heat and gradually add a ladleful into the egg mixture, whisking well. Gradually add 2 more ladles while whisking, then pour back into the pan. Heat over low-medium heat, stirring, until thickened enough to easily coat the back of a wooden spoon. Do not let it boil. Pour it immediately through a fine strainer into a bowl. Put the vanilla bean back into the custard. Let the mixture cool, then refrigerate for 2 hours or overnight to thicken. Pull out the vanilla bean and scrape the remaining seeds into the custard.

Pour the mixture into your ice pop molds, leaving ¼-inch at the top to let the mixture expand when it freezes. Insert the ice pop sticks and freeze. (See page 22 for the complete procedure.) To dip the ice pops in the white and dark chocolates, see page 20.

CARAMEL CHOCOLATE

This is Cesar's indulgent recipe for a caramel ice pop, which, great as it is, tastes even better dipped in chocolate and almonds.

- scant 1 cup granulated sugar
- 2¼ cups whole milk
- generous 1 cup heavy cream
- 3 egg yolks
- ¼ teaspoon vanilla extract
- a pinch of salt

Place a heavy saucepan over medium heat. Once hot, pour the sugar in and shake the pan, stirring with a wooden spoon until the sugar has melted. When the sugar starts to color, it will caramelize and the temperature will rise very quickly, so watch it! Do not burn it or it will become bitter. As soon as it's golden amber, remove the pan from the heat. Add the milk and cream straightaway, but be very careful because it will splutter. Put the mixture back over the heat and bring to a simmer, stirring to dissolve the hardened caramel.

In a large bowl, briefly whisk together the egg yolks, vanilla, and salt. Remove the pan from the heat and gradually whisk the hot caramel into the eggs, then transfer everything back into the pan. Heat again over medium heat, stirring constantly until the mixture thickens enough to easily coat the back of a wooden spoon. Do not let it boil! Strain the mixture into a clean bowl and place the bowl over ice to cool it quickly. Now refrigerate it until chilled.

Pour the mixture into your ice pop molds, leaving ¼-inch at the top to let the mixture expand when it freezes. Insert the ice pop sticks and freeze. (See page 22 for the complete procedure.) To cap the frozen ice pops with chocolate, see page 20, adding chopped almonds to the melted chocolate.

MEXICAN CHOCOLATE

Inspired by the Aztecs' chocolate and chili drink, this is an intriguing combination that we can't get enough of.

- 2¼ cups whole milk
- generous 1 cup heavy cream
- 1 cinnamon stick, broken up
- 3-5 generous pinches of cayenne pepper, plus optional extra to sprinkle on the ice pops
- 5½ ounces dark chocolate, finely chopped
- ¼ cup plus 2 tablespoons granulated sugar

Put the milk, cream, cinnamon stick, and cayenne pepper in a medium saucepan and bring to a simmer. Simmer for 5 minutes. Remove the pan from the heat, add the chocolate and sugar, and stir until well blended and creamy.

Set the mixture aside to cool and to let the flavors infuse. The longer it sits, the smoother and creamier your ice pop will be. We sometimes let it sit overnight.

Strain the mixture through a fine strainer, then pour it into your ice pop molds, leaving ¼-inch at the top to let the mixture expand when it freezes. Insert the ice pop sticks and freeze. (See page 22 for the complete procedure.) Sprinkle just a tiny bit of extra cayenne pepper on the frozen ice pops, if you like.

CHOCOLATE & VANILLA SWIRL

Sicilians use cornstarch as a thickener in their ice cream—it allows the flavors to shine through and it gives a good texture. Here we use it to add a nice chewy bite to the ice pop. If you like a deeper chocolate, use the cocoa in addition to the dark chocolate.

- 2¼ cups whole milk
- scant ¼ cup cornstarch
- generous 1 cup heavy cream
- 2 teaspoons vanilla extract
- 6 tablespoons granulated sugar
- 3½ ounces dark chocolate, finely chopped
- 4 teaspoons unsweetened cocoa powder mixed with 3 tablespoons hot water (optional)

Put 3 tablespoons of the milk in a small bowl and mix in the cornstarch to form a smooth paste. Pour the remaining milk and the cream in a medium saucepan and heat until just about to simmer, then stir in the cornstarch paste. Stir constantly until the mixture starts to thicken and bubble. Let thicken, stirring, for an additional 2 minutes.

Pour the mixture through a fine strainer and divide between 2 bowls. Stir half the vanilla and 4 tablespoons of the sugar into one bowl; and stir the remaining vanilla and remaining sugar plus the chocolate into the second bowl until smooth and well blended. If you are using the cocoa mixture, stir it into the chocolate bowl. Let the mixtures cool to room temperature.

Spoon alternate vanilla and chocolate layers in your ice pop molds, leaving ¼-inch at the top to let the mixture expand when it freezes. Insert ice pop sticks and freeze. (See page 22 for the procedure.)

CHOCOLATE

This recipe gives you the perfect chocolate ice pop that you can enjoy—pure and simple. It can also be transformed with other flavorings, such as orange, rosemary, rose, or coffee (see Variations below).

- 2¼ cups whole milk
- generous 1 cup heavy cream
- 5½ ounces good-quality dark chocolate, finely chopped
- scant ⅓-generous ⅓ cup granulated sugar (depending on the sweetness of your chocolate)
- 2 teaspoons vanilla extract

Put the milk and cream in a saucepan and bring to a simmer. Remove the pan from the heat, add the chocolate and sugar, and stir until well blended and creamy. Stir in the vanilla. Set the mixture aside to cool. The longer it sits, the smoother and creamier your ice pop will be.

Pour the mixture into your ice pop molds, leaving ¼-inch at the top to let the mixture expand when it freezes. Insert the ice pop sticks and freeze. (See page 22 for the complete procedure.)

If you like, you can artfully drip some melted dark chocolate over the ice pop (see page 20 for help with melting chocolate).

Variations:
For orange chocolate, add 2 teaspoons finely grated orange zest; for rose chocolate, add 2 teaspoons rosewater; for rosemary chocolate, add a few sprigs of fresh rosemary to the milk as it simmers and pull them out just before freezing. For those who love mocha, stir in 2 teaspoons instant coffee at the same time as the chocolate.

CAPPUCCINO

Use really fresh, dark roast coffee and make it extra strong for this cappuccino-on-a-stick. We use a ceramic coffee dripper with a paper cone right over a cup. If you have an espresso machine, that's even better.

- scant ⅓ cup granulated sugar
- 2¼ cups freshly brewed, extra strong coffee
- generous 1 cup whipping cream
- 1–2 tablespoons superfine sugar
- 1–2 drops of vanilla extract (optional)
- cocoa powder, ground cinnamon, or grated nutmeg to sprinkle on the ice pops

Add the granulated sugar to the freshly brewed coffee and stir until the sugar has dissolved. Stir in half the cream until it's well blended.

Put the remaining cream, superfine sugar, and vanilla, if using, in a bowl and beat until slightly firm.

Pour the coffee mixture into your ice pop molds—there should be some room left for the cream. Spoon the cream on top, leaving ¼-inch at the top to let the mixture expand when it freezes. Insert the ice pop sticks and freeze. (See page 22 for the complete procedure.) Sprinkle unsweetened cocoa powder, ground cinnamon, or grated nutmeg over the frozen ice pops, if you like.

VIETNAMESE COFFEE

As young artists in New York, we used to go around the corner to a Vietnamese restaurant called Nha Trang in Chinatown for cheap and delicious meals. They used to bring each of us a cup with sweet condensed milk in the bottom and then brewed a coffee through a small metal filter individually over each cup. The whole ceremony made a big impression. Here it is, on a stick. To brew the strong coffee needed for this ice pop, we use a paper filter directly over a cup and load it with coffee grounds. You'll be flying.

- $^2/_3$ cup sweetened condensed milk
- $2^1/_4$ cups freshly brewed, extra strong coffee (the very strongest you can make!)
- scant $^1/_2$ cup heavy cream

Put the condensed milk into a bowl and pour the freshly brewed coffee and the cream over it. Mix until completely blended.

Pour the mixture into your ice pop molds, leaving $^1/_4$-inch at the top to let the mixture expand when it freezes. Insert the ice pop sticks and freeze. (See page 22 for the complete procedure.)

EARL GREY

Earl Grey, the British prime minister in the 1830s, reportedly received this blend of tea as a gift from a Chinese Mandarin. The tea is distinctively scented with the oil of the bergamot orange.

- 2¼ cups whole milk
- scant ¼ cup cornstarch
- generous 1 cup heavy cream
- scant ⅔ cup granulated sugar
- 5 teaspoons Earl Grey tea leaves
- 1 teaspoon vanilla extract (optional)

Put 3 tablespoons of the milk in a small bowl and mix in the cornstarch to form a smooth paste. Pour the remaining milk, the cream, and sugar in a medium saucepan and heat until just about to boil, then remove the pan from the heat and stir in the tea leaves. Let steep for 5 minutes.

Stir in the cornstarch paste and return the pan to the heat. Stir constantly until the mixture starts to thicken and bubble. Let thicken, stirring constantly, for an additional 2 minutes.

Pour the mixture through a fine strainer, pressing down on the leaves with the back of a spoon to extract the flavor. Stir in the vanilla, if using, and let cool to room temperature.

Pour the mixture into your ice pop molds, leaving ¼-inch at the top to let the mixture expand when it freezes. Insert the ice pop sticks and freeze. (See page 22 for the complete procedure.)

Variation:
You can substitute another highly fragrant tea leaf for the Earl Grey.

CUCUMBER & LIME

This refreshing and intense ice pop is perfect for a break during a sweltering day or for a warm summer evening outside. The skin of the cucumber is where the nutrients are stored and is also what gives this ice pop its jade green color, so don't remove it!

- 1 large English cucumber, rinsed
- generous 1 cup water
- 1/3 cup freshly squeezed lime juice (from about 2-3 limes)
- 1/2 cup granulated sugar

Leave the skin on the cucumber. Cut off the ends and slice the cucumber thickly. Put the cucumber and water in a food processor and blend to a fine puree.

Strain the puree through a fine strainer and add the lime juice and sugar. Stir until the sugar has dissolved.

Pour the mixture into your ice pop molds, leaving 1/4-inch at the top to let the mixture expand when it freezes. Insert the ice pop sticks and freeze. (See page 22 for the complete procedure.)

BEET & SOUR CREAM

Be prepared for a pair of beautifully stained magenta lips after eating this! This Russian-inspired ice pop is also full of health benefits. It's easiest to use fresh store-bought beet juice but you can make your own, of course. If you do, be sure to keep the skins on when you run them through the juicer, since that is where most of the nutrients are stored.

- 2¼ cups fresh beet juice
- 2 tablespoons freshly squeezed lemon juice
- 2 tablespoons superfine sugar
- generous 1 cup sour cream

Mix together the beet and lemon juices and sugar. Stir until the sugar has dissolved. Stir in the sour cream until well blended.

Pour the mixture into your ice pop molds, leaving ¼-inch at the top to let the mixture expand when it freezes. Insert the ice pop sticks and freeze. (See page 22 for the complete procedure.)

INDEX

A
alcohol 16
almonds: almond & orange blossom 84
  cassata 98
apricot & pistachio 50

B
bananas: banana chocodip 68
  cereal milk 104
basil, cantaloupe & 38
beet & sour cream 124
berry, Burgundy 78
blackberry 32
blueberry & yogurt 48
Burgundy berry 78
butterscotch 100

C
Campari, ruby grapefruit & 54
candied peel: cassata 98
cantaloupe & basil 38
cappuccino 116
caramel: butterscotch 100
  caramel chocolate 108
cassata 98
cereal milk 104
cheesecake, 50s orange 94
cherry & red currant 58
chocolate 114
  banana chocodip 68
  caramel chocolate 108
  cassata 98
  chocolate & vanilla swirl 112
  coating ice pops 20
  Mexican chocolate 110
  mocha 114
  New York black & white 106
  orange chocolate 114
  rose chocolate 114
  rosemary chocolate 114
clementine, white wine & rose 62
coconut milk: coconut & lime 66
  pineapple & coconut 64
coffee: cappuccino 116
  mocha 114
  Vietnamese coffee 118
cranberry & orange 70
cream 16
cucumber & lime 122
custard, rhubarb & 72

D
decorations 20
drenched watermelon 42

E
Earl Grey 120
Egyptian hibiscus & peach 76
equipment 17

F
50s orange cheesecake 94
freezing ice pops 22
French twist 92
fruit 16

G
ginger: lemon & ginger 30
  sweet pear & ginger 56
grapefruit: ruby grapefruit & Campari 54
  white grapefruit & star anise 74
greengage plum 36

H
herbs 16
hibiscus & peach 76
honey 16
  cereal milk 104
  milk & honey 96

K
kulfi, Soni's 102

L
lemon juice 16
  lemon & ginger 30
  orange & lemon 26
  three milks lemon dessert 90
lemongrass, lychee & 40
lime juice 16
  coconut & lime 66
  cucumber & lime 122
  drenched watermelon 42
  mojito 80
  raspberry & lime 28
lychee & lemongrass 40

M
mango, fresh 60
maple syrup 16
melon: cantaloupe & basil 38
Mexican chocolate 110
milk 16

cereal milk 104
milk & honey 96
minted milk 88
Soni's kulfi 102
three milks lemon
    dessert 90
mint: minted milk 88
    mojito 80
mocha 114
mojito 80
molds 18, 22, 23

N
New York black &
    white 106
nuts, toasting 20

O
orange blossom,
    almond & 84
orange juice:
    cranberry &
        orange 70
    50s orange
        cheesecake 94
    orange & lemon 26
    orange chocolate
        114

P
peaches: Egyptian
    hibiscus & peach
    76
    peach & tarragon 52
    peaches & cream 46
pears: sweet pear &
    ginger 56
pepper, strawberry &
    44
pineapple & coconut
    64
pistachios: apricot &
    pistachio 50
    cassata 98
    pistachio & rose 86
    Soni's kulfi 102
plum, tart 36

R
raisins, sweet sherry
    & 82
raspberries: French
    twist 92
    raspberry & lime 28
red currant, cherry &
    58
rhubarb & custard 72
ricotta: cassata 98
rosewater:
    clementine, white
        wine & rose 62
    pistachio & rose 86
    rose chocolate 114
rosemary chocolate
    114
ruby grapefruit &
    Campari 54
rum: mojito 80

S
salt 16
sherry & raisin 82
Soni's kulfi 102
sour cream, beet
    & 124
spices 16
sprinkles 20
star anise, white
    grapefruit & 74
sticks 18, 22
storing ice pops 23
strawberries:
    strawberries &
        cream 34
    strawberry & pepper
        44
stripes 19
sugar 16
suspending
    ingredients 19
sweetness 16
swirls 19

T
tarragon, peach & 52
tart plum 36
tea: Earl Grey 120
techniques 15-23
three milks lemon
    dessert 90
toasting nuts 20
transporting ice pops
    23

V
vanilla: cassata 98
    chocolate & vanilla
        swirl 112
    French twist 92
    New York black &
        white 106
Vietnamese coffee 118

W
watermelon, drenched
    42
white grapefruit &
    star anise 74
wine: Burgundy berry
    78
    clementine, white
        wine & rose 62
wooden sticks 18

Y
yogurt 16
    blueberry &
        yogurt 48

127

ACKNOWLEDGMENTS

We'd like to thank everyone at Quadrille for the idea of making this book and giving us so much freedom to do it: Ed and Simon for their enthusiasm and vision, Jane for her wise guidance throughout, Helen for her exceptional eye, Gemma for making it look this beautiful, and Céline for her sensitive editing. Special thanks to Lizzy Kremer, our awesome agent.

Thank you, Lily, for being the biggest inspiration and for being our ultimate taste tester. We thank Claudia who taught us the pleasures of cooking and who is always there for us; Paul for his belief and encouragement to always follow our dreams and to shoot from the hip; Peggy for getting caught up in this ice pop madness, and for all her hard work. A big thank you to Peter for designing the book and striking cover, his girlfriend Divya Scialo for helping with line illustrations, and our friend Adam Slama for photographing all the ice pops so beautifully.

A massive thank you to Simon and Ros for helping to set up the Ice Kitchen at their home last year and making it all possible, and for putting up with all the endless crates of fruit.

Special thanks to Sybil for her generous spirit; Tom for the website, Chantal for her sound advice; and our families and Gemma and Terry for being the ice pop guinea pigs, even when they didn't turn out so well and didn't make it into the book. Thank you all for your love and support.